Wi iaLS

EMILY FELLAH

Brimming with creative inspiration, how-to projects, and useful information to enrich your everyday life, Quarto Knows is a favorite destination for those pursuing their interests and passions. Visit our site and dig deeper with our books into your area of interest: Quarto Creates, Quarto Cooks, Quarto Homes, Quarto Lives, Quarto Drives, Quarto Explores, Quarto Gifts, or Quarto Kids.

© 2021 Quarto Publishing Group USA Inc.
Text and illustrations © 2021 Emily Fellah

First published in 2021 by Walter Foster Jr., an imprint of The Quarto Group.
26391 Crown Valley Parkway, Suite 220, Mission Viejo, CA 92691, USA.
T (949) 380-7510 **F** (949) 380-7575 **www.QuartoKnows.com**

Walter Foster Jr. titles are also available at discount for retail, wholesale, promotional, and bulk purchase. For details, contact the Special Sales Manager by email at specialsales@quarto.com or by mail at The Quarto Group, Attn: Special Sales Manager, 100 Cummings Center, Suite 265D, Beverly, MA 01915, USA.

ISBN: 978-1-60058-938-6

Digital edition published in 2021
eISBN: 978-1-60058-956-0

Printed in China
10 9 8 7 6 5 4 3 2 1

MIX
Paper from
responsible sources
FSC® C016973

TABLE OF CONTENTS

How to Use This Book 4

Lion. 6

Elephant 8

Bear 10

Deer 12

Hedgehog 14

Whale. 15

Panda. 16

Badger 18

Tortoise 19

Chimpanzee 20

Giraffe 22

Rhinoceros 24

Tiger 26

Wolf 28

Zebra 30

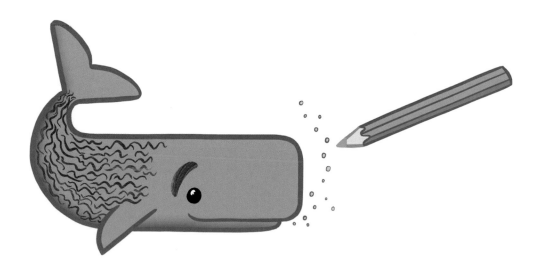

Step-by-Step Drawing

This book contains 15 fun drawing projects with step-by-step instructions. Each new step is in color, making it easy to follow along.

Top Tips

Start lightly in pencil because you will be erasing some of the lines that helped to build your character.

Be careful when erasing because you don't want to crumple or tear your drawing.

If you'd like, you can draw over your finished characters with a fine-line pen or felt-tip marker and erase your pencil lines when the ink is dry.

Tools & Materials

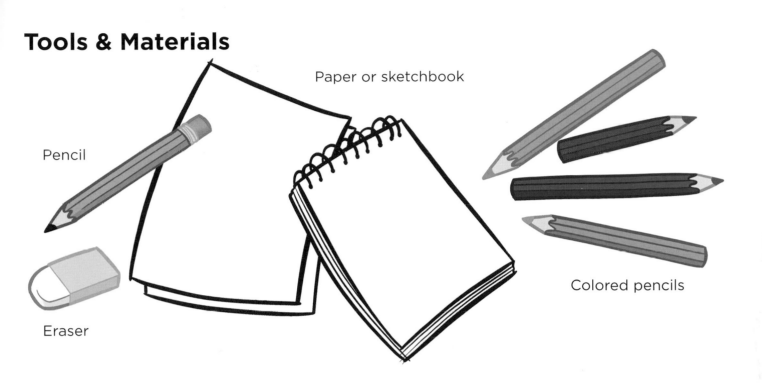

Paper or sketchbook

Pencil

Eraser

Colored pencils

Extras Fine-line pen or felt-tip marker, colored pens, crayons

You Are an Artist!

Your drawings will turn out a little differently from the ones in the book, which is a good thing. You are an individual, and your art will reflect your style and personality, so be proud of it!

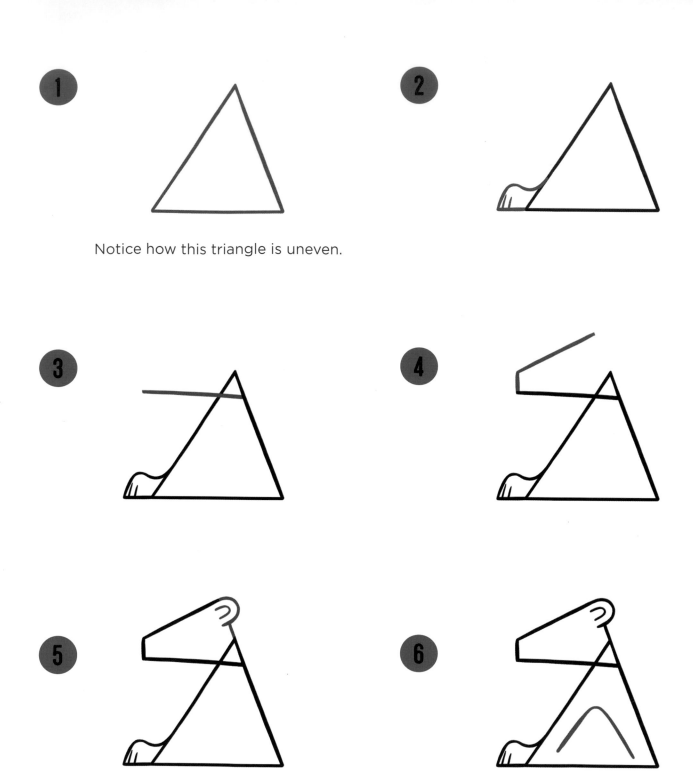

1 Notice how this triangle is uneven.

5 Draw the ear first. Then draw a line to meet your original triangle.

7

8

9

10

Draw the mane, and then erase the lines you don't need anymore.

11

12

It's coloring time!

ELEPHANT

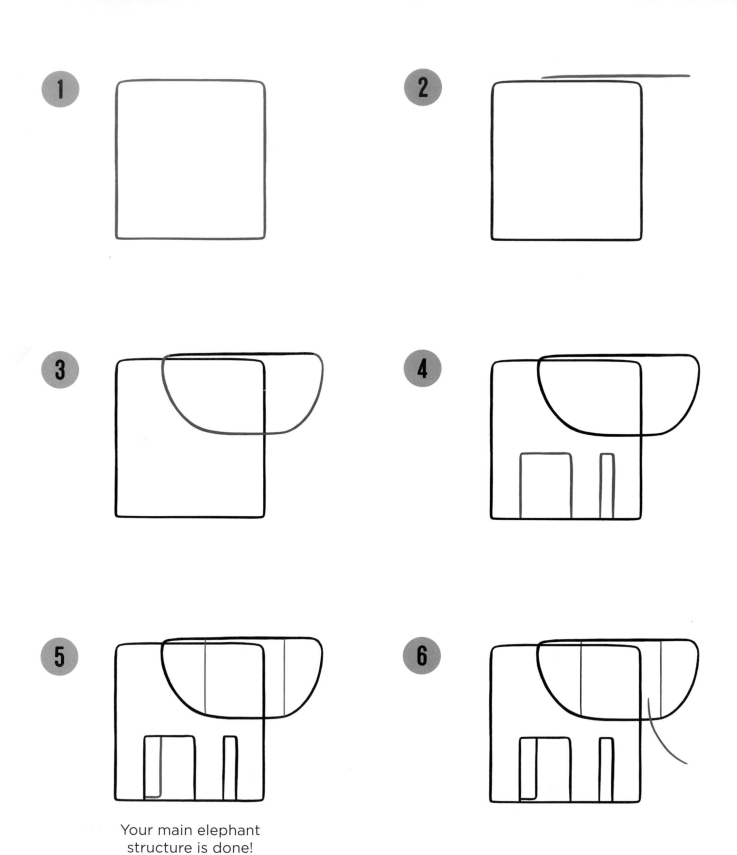

1

2

3

4

5

6

Your main elephant
structure is done!

7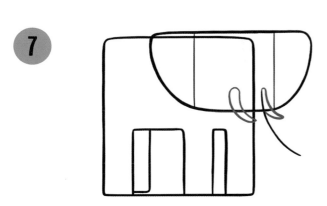

8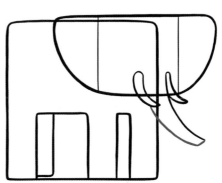

9

Erase any lines you don't need anymore.
Then draw the eyes and eyebrows.

10

11

12

Add some color, if you'd like.

9

BEAR

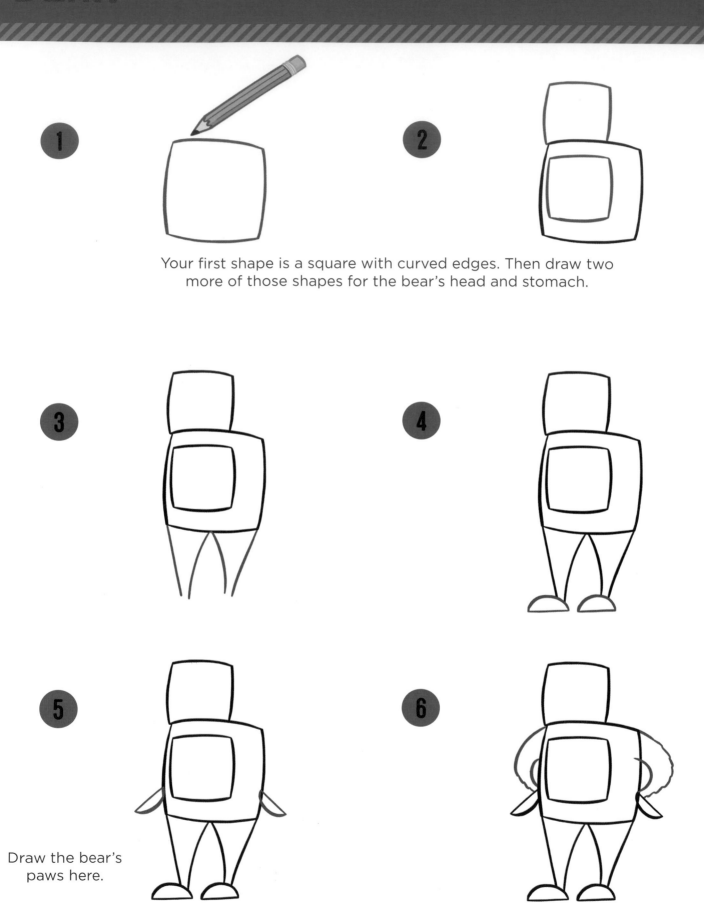

1 Your first shape is a square with curved edges. Then draw two more of those shapes for the bear's head and stomach.

2

3

4

5 Draw the bear's paws here.

6

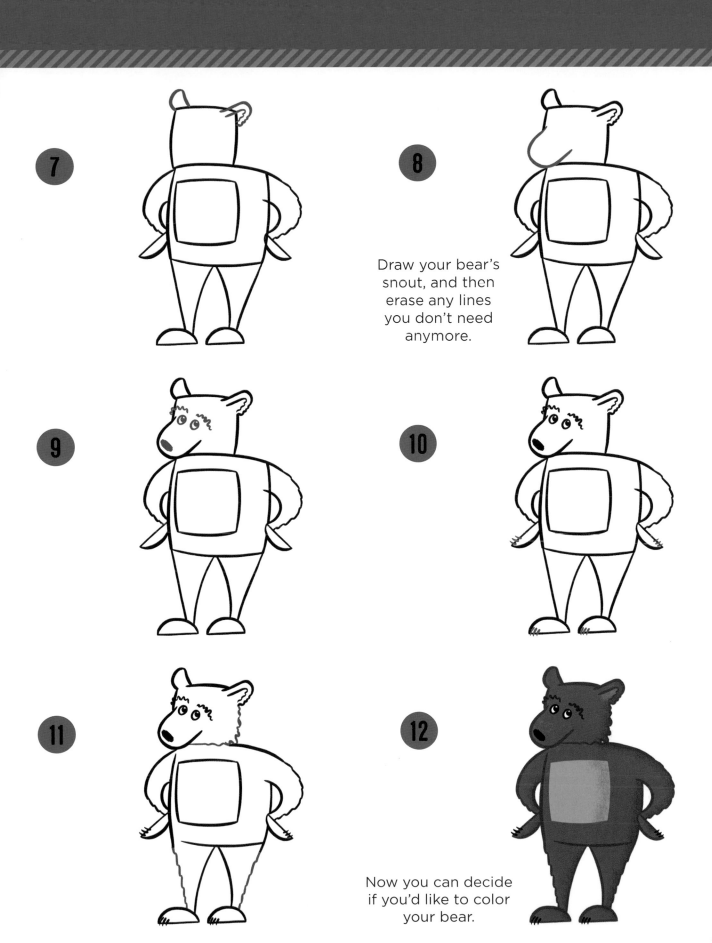

7

8

Draw your bear's snout, and then erase any lines you don't need anymore.

9

10

11

12

Now you can decide if you'd like to color your bear.

DEER

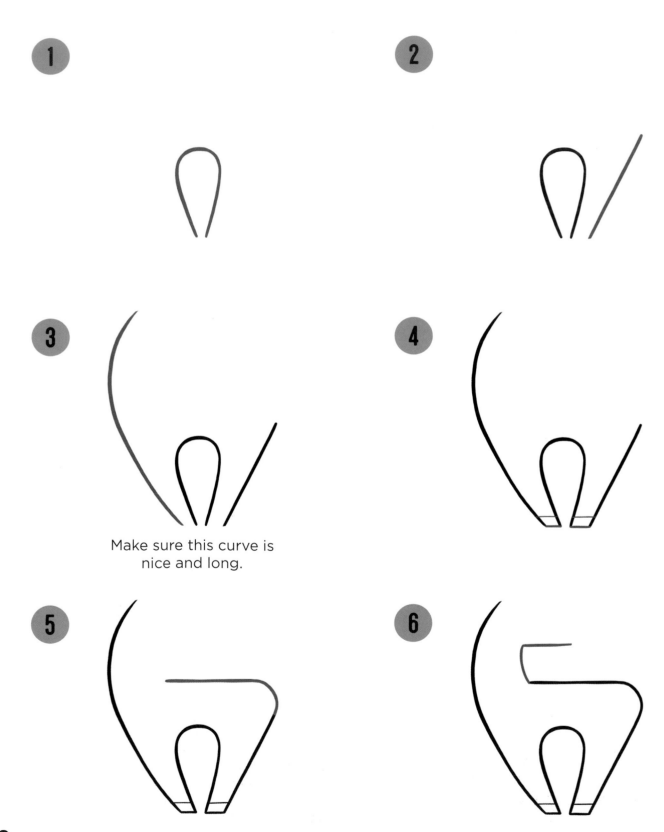

1

2

3

Make sure this curve is
nice and long.

4

5

6

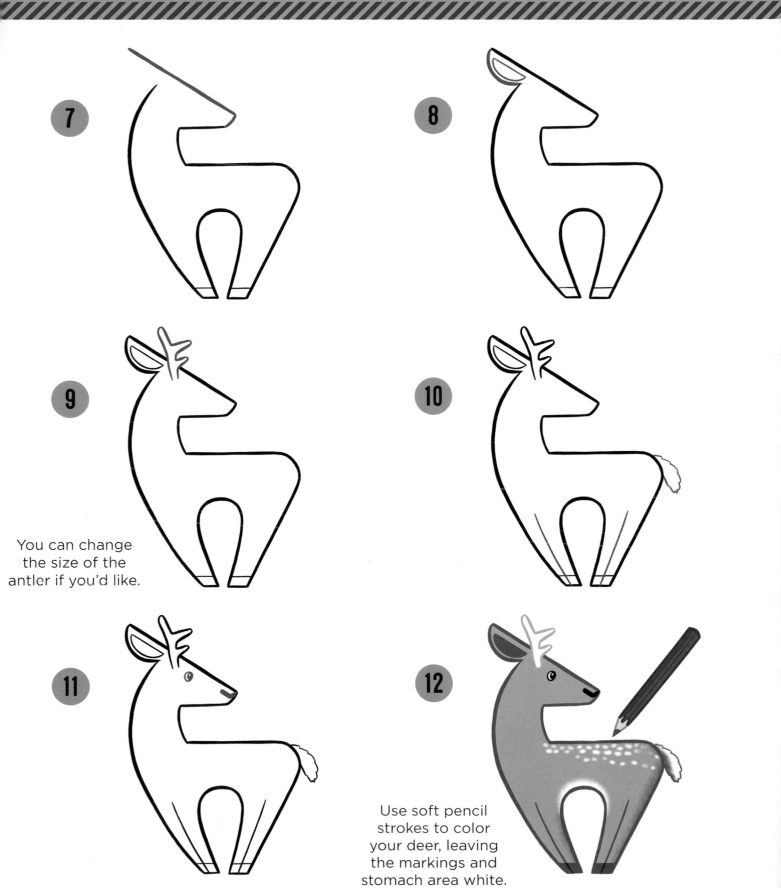

7

8

9

You can change
the size of the
antler if you'd like.

10

11

12

Use soft pencil
strokes to color
your deer, leaving
the markings and
stomach area white.

1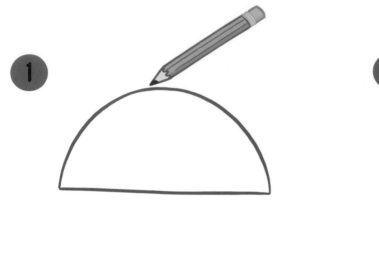

2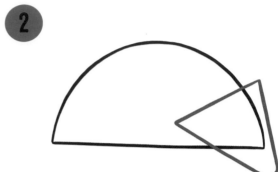

3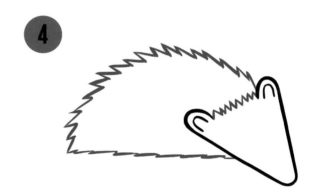

4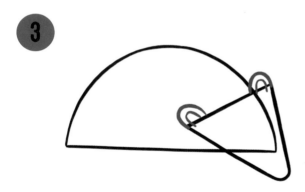

Draw the spikes and head shape in pen, and then gently erase your pencil lines.

5

6

Use pencil for the feet, claws, and face. Then draw over them in pen and add color.

WHALE

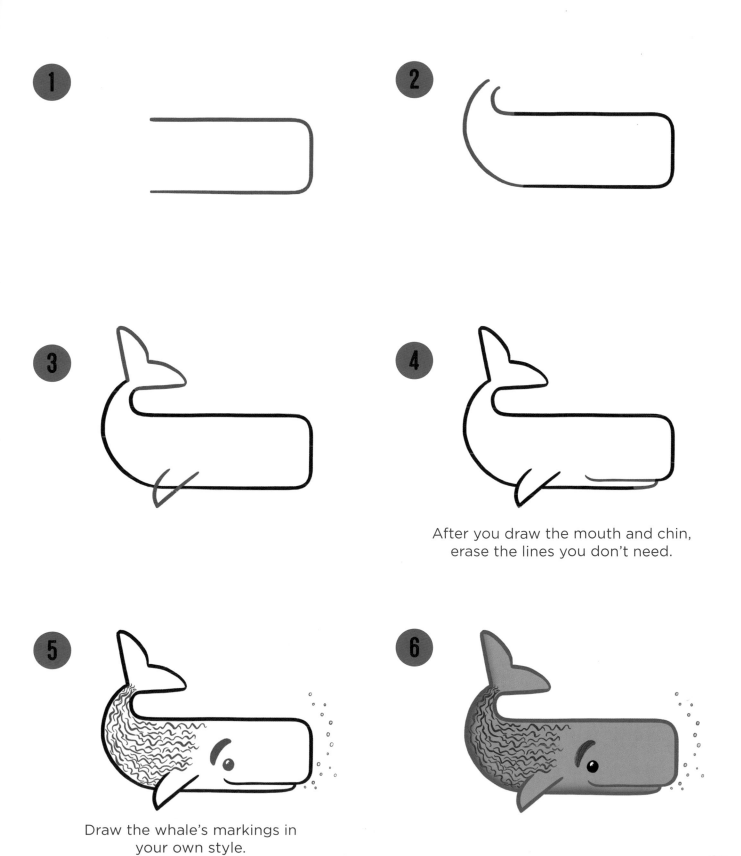

4

After you draw the mouth and chin, erase the lines you don't need.

5

Draw the whale's markings in your own style.

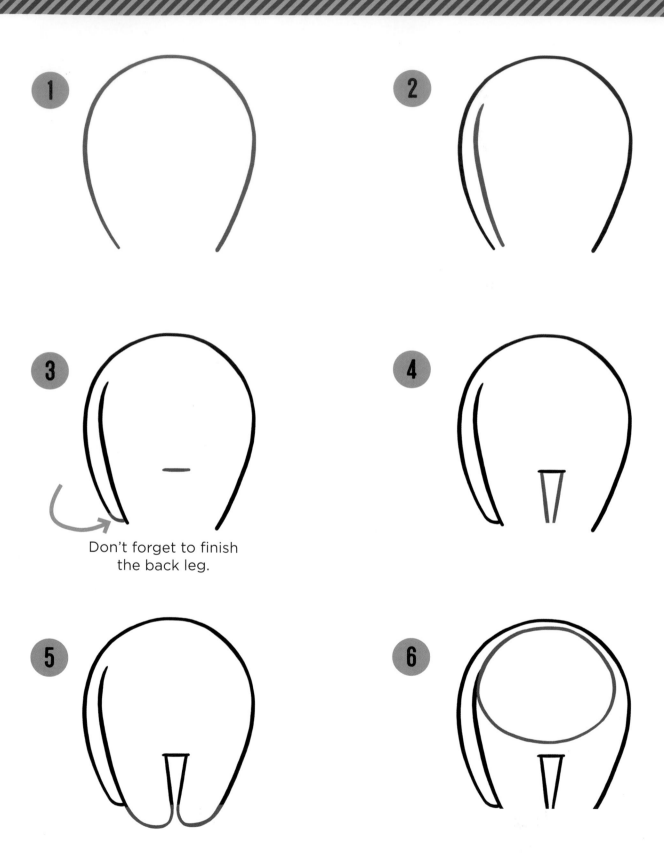

Don't forget to finish the back leg.

7

The panda's snout is
a simple circle.

8

9

10

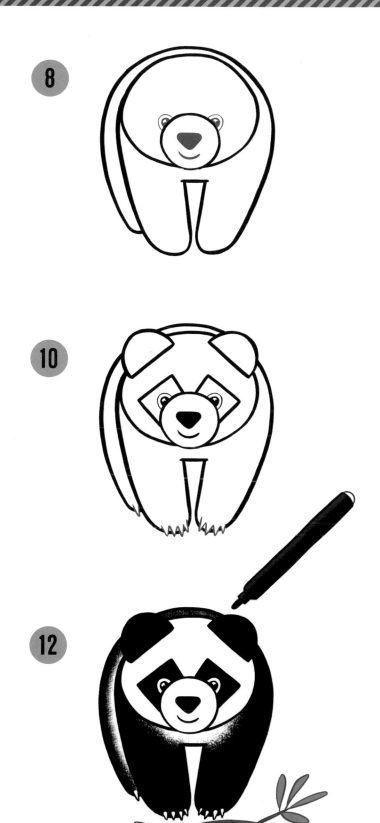

11

Color the eye patches, ears, and much of
the body black, leaving some white. Then
add some bamboo if you'd like.

12

BADGER

1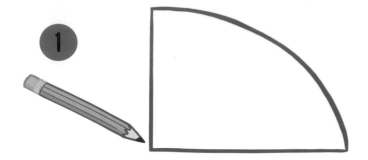

2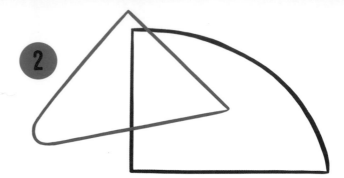

Take your time with the head shape.

3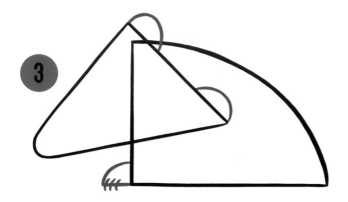

4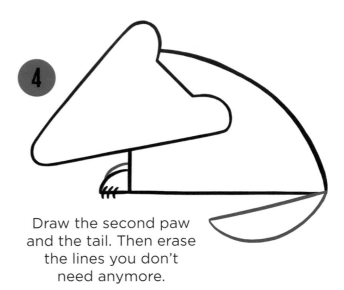

Draw the second paw and the tail. Then erase the lines you don't need anymore.

5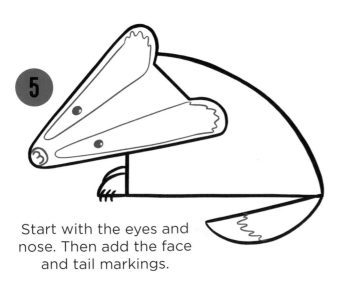

Start with the eyes and nose. Then add the face and tail markings.

6

You could color the body a solid black or leave the fur lines white.

1

2

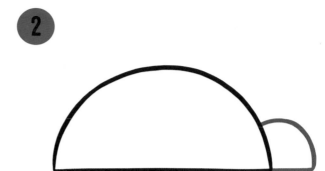

3

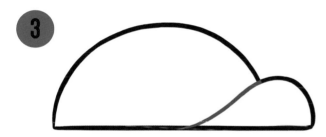

Once you've drawn this curve, you can erase the line that goes through the head.

4

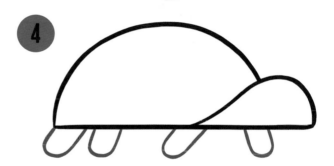

5

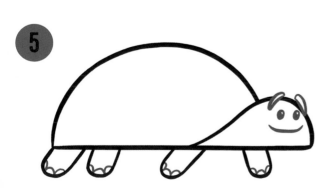

6

Create your own unique shell pattern.

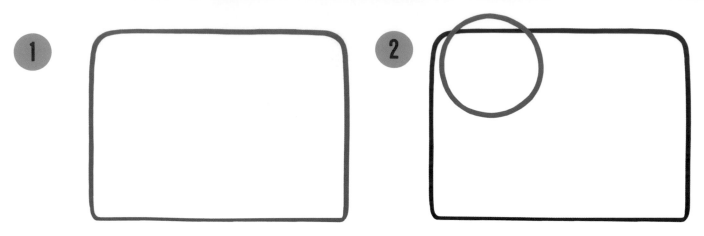

1 Start this chimpanzee by drawing a large rectangle with rounded corners at the top.

2

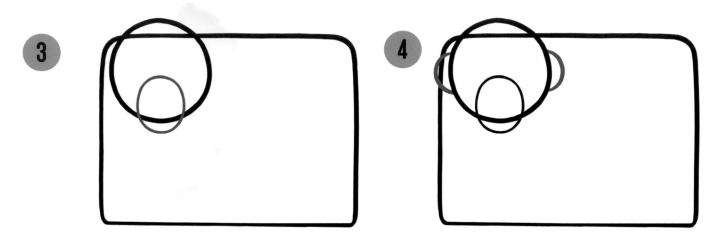

3

4

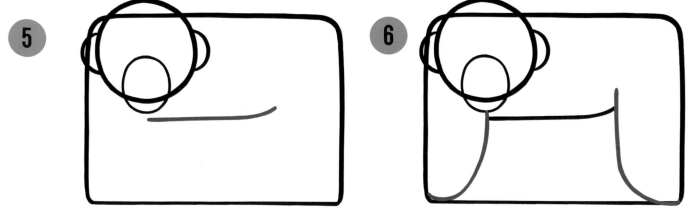

5

6 These curved lines make up an arm and a leg.

7

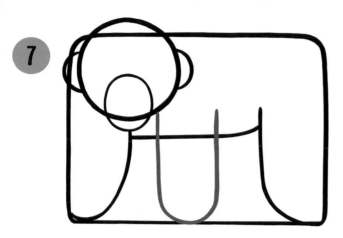

Draw this arm fairly close to the first arm.

8

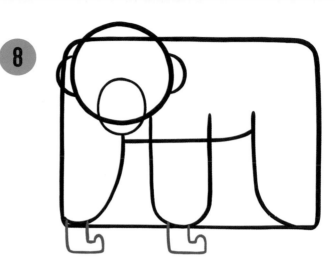

9

Gently erase the lines you don't need anymore and draw the foot.

10

11

12

GIRAFFE

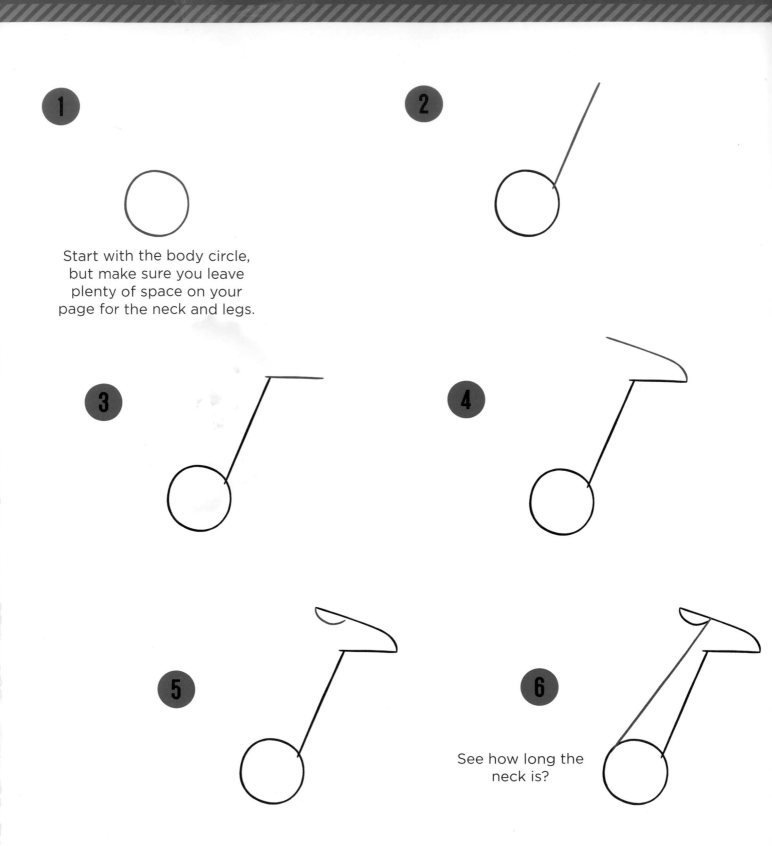

1

Start with the body circle, but make sure you leave plenty of space on your page for the neck and legs.

2

3

4

5

6

See how long the neck is?

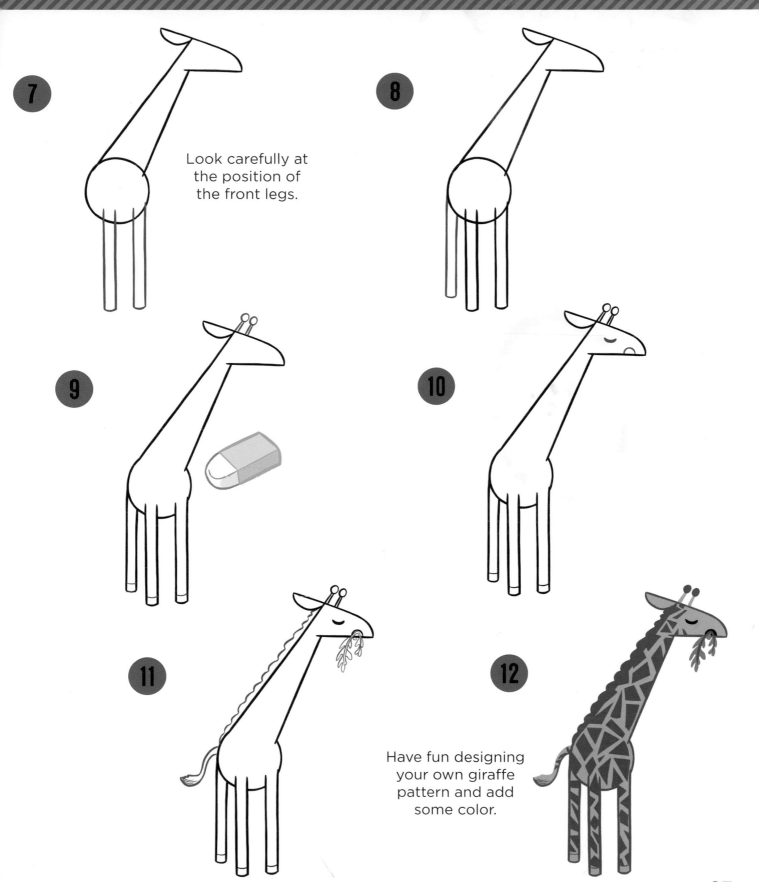

7

8

Look carefully at
the position of
the front legs.

9

10

11

12

Have fun designing
your own giraffe
pattern and add
some color.

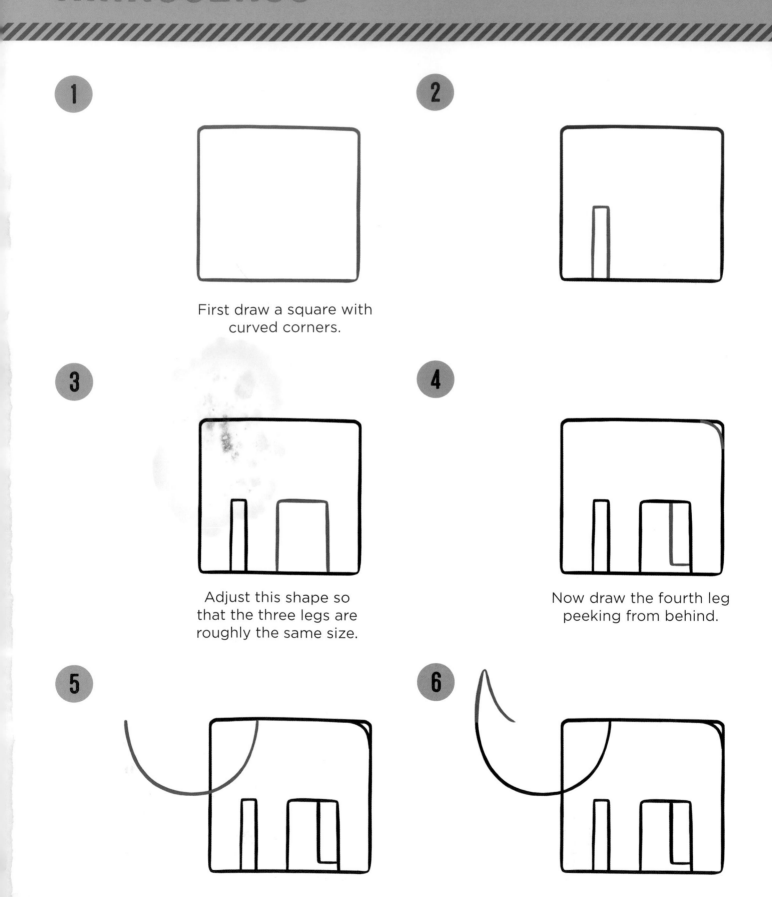

1 First draw a square with curved corners.

2

3 Adjust this shape so that the three legs are roughly the same size.

4 Now draw the fourth leg peeking from behind.

5

6

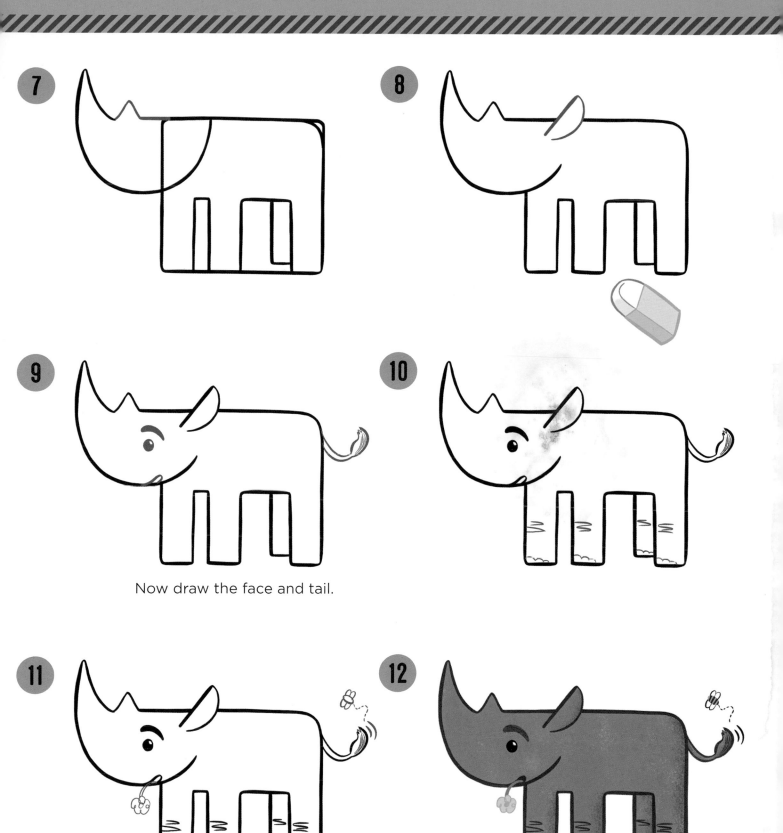

Now draw the face and tail.

TIGER

1

Start lightly in pencil and take your time to get this shape right.

2

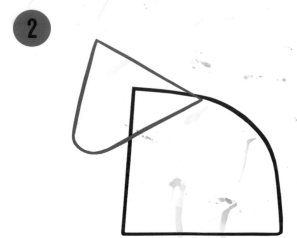

3

4

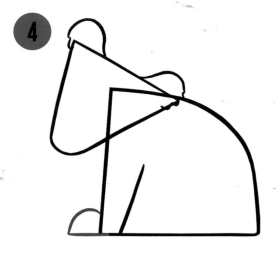

5

6

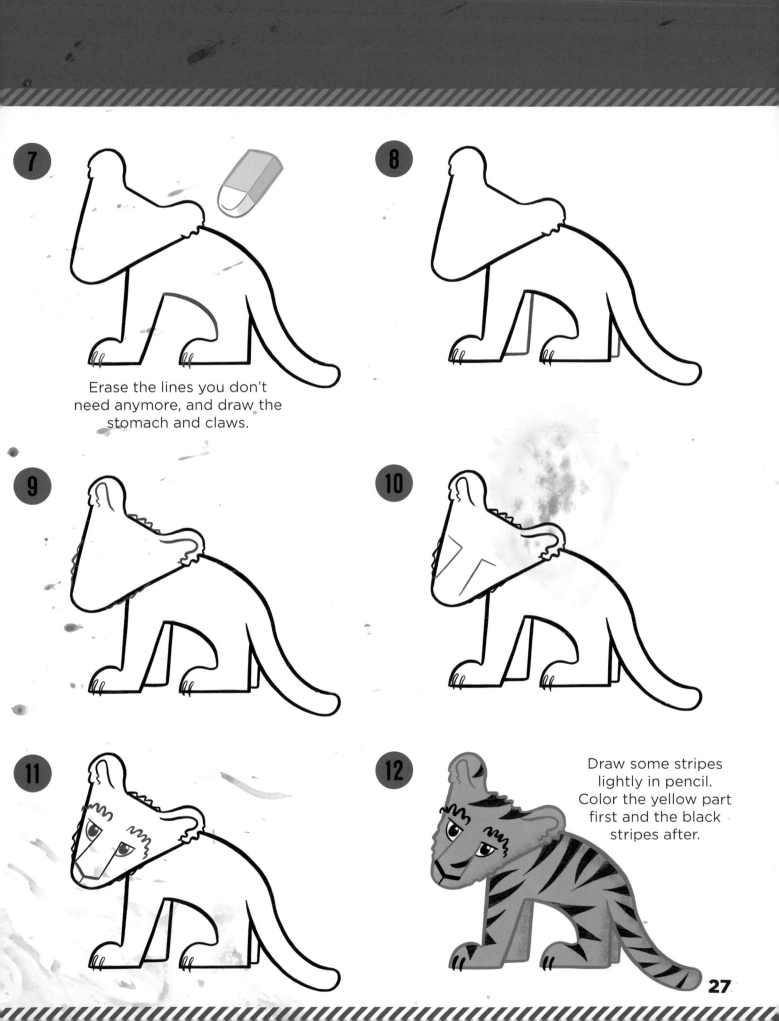

7 Erase the lines you don't need anymore, and draw the stomach and claws.

8

9

10

11

12 Draw some stripes lightly in pencil. Color the yellow part first and the black stripes after.

WOLF

1

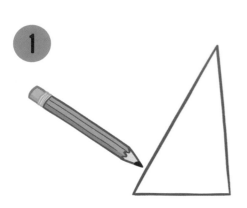

2

3

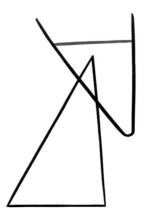

4

5

Adjust your lines so that you're happy with the size of the ears.

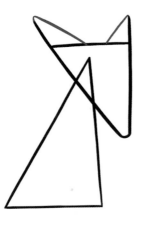

6

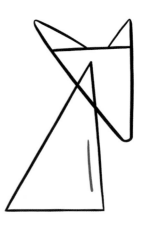

7

8

9

10

Add some more furry lines and erase the lines you don't need anymore.

11

12

Leave some white patches when you color.

ZEBRA

1

Draw this circle in the
middle of your page so that
you don't run out of space.

2

3

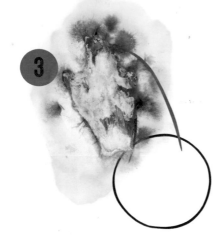

4

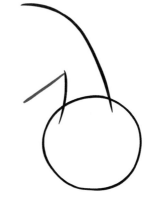

5

Adjust your lines now if
the head shape doesn't
look quite right.

6

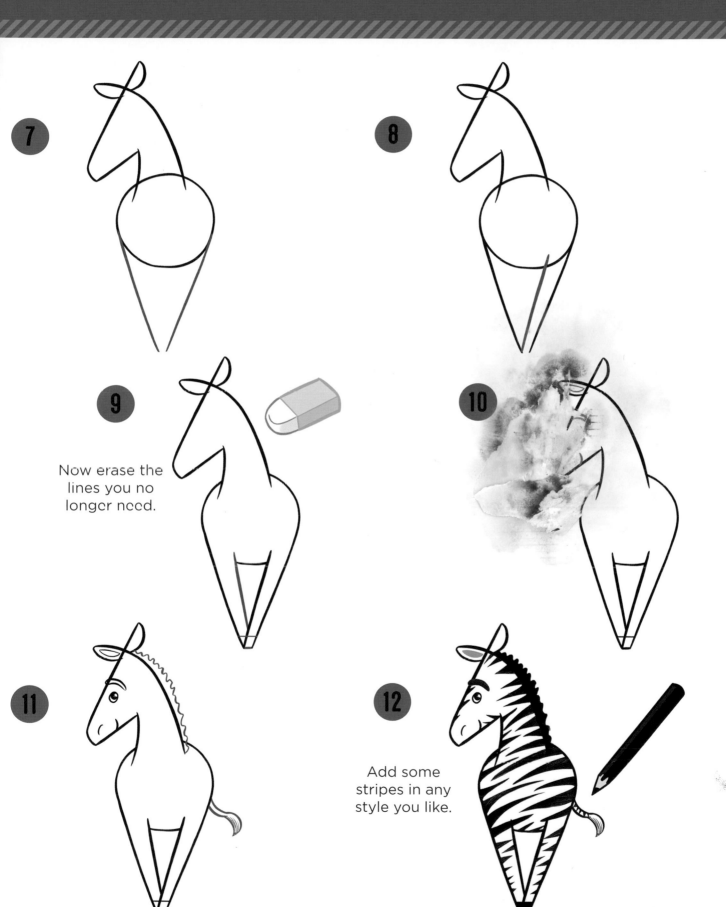

7

8

9

Now erase the lines you no longer need.

10

11

12

Add some stripes in any style you like.

Also available in this series ...

I Can Draw: Favorite Pets
ISBN: 978-1-60058-939-3

I Can Draw: Cats & Kittens
ISBN: 978-1-60058-958-4

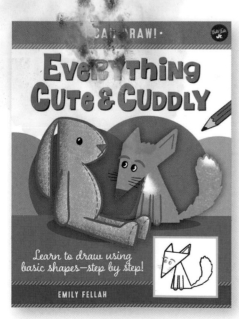

I Can Draw: Everything Cute & Cuddly
ISBN: 978-1-60058-960-7

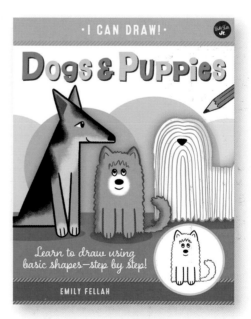

I Can Draw: Dogs & Puppies
ISBN: 978-1-60058-962-1